Wolfie
and *Me*

by
Audrey Magnant
Williams

TEACH Services, Inc.
P U B L I S H I N G
www.TEACHServices.com • (800) 367-1844

I0141013

Copyright © 2016 TEACH Services, Inc.
ISBN-13: 978-1-4796-0641-2 (Paperback)
ISBN-13: 978-1-4796-0642-9 (ePub)
ISBN-13: 978-1-4796-0643-6 (Mobi)

Published by

TEACH Services, Inc.
P U B L I S H I N G
www.TEACHServices.com • (800) 367-1844

Dedicated to my two younger brothers
Keith and Earl Magnant, for their part
in the making of this book.

Years ago our neighbor brought his funny-looking little dog to our house and asked Mama if he could leave her there a few days. Mama said yes. Mama was always willing to help anyone in trouble. But she had no idea how long "a few days" meant to Bob—or how much joy and how much tragedy that dog would bring to our family.

Bob had picked the dog up on one of his trips to Arkansas, so he had named her Arkie. She was a mixture of some kind of terrier and who knows what else. She made herself right at home. I always thought she was rather homely, but Rex, our little Shetland sheepdog, must have thought otherwise. Soon we had three fat little puppies to add to our collection of farm animals. They included two horses, one cow, now five dogs, some cats, and a herd of goats. That didn't include the chickens.

Of course, my two younger brothers, Keith and Earl, and I would have loved to keep all three puppies, but Mama was firm. She allowed us to pick one puppy, and the other two found new homes.

Picking out just one puppy was no problem for us. One was different from the other two. He loved to wrestle, play, and growl. He had a line of hair on his back that would stand straight up when he got excited. He looked and acted more like a wolf puppy than a dog, so we named him Wolfie.

Months passed, and Bob still hadn't returned to pick up Arkie. No one else wanted her, so she stayed. Then a strange thing happened. One day she took Wolfie across the road to the barnyard and started his training as a herd dog. She taught him to take the goats out to pasture and bring them back to the barn at milking time. She allowed no mistakes. If he didn't obey, she would nip him on the leg. It was funny to watch this bigger dog taking orders from his smaller mother. Eventually, Wolfie became an expert at herding and even learned to enjoy his job.

Then things changed. Bob returned, and Arkie was gone, leaving a hollow spot in our lives. Wolfie didn't understand. He looked all over for his mother. He searched the house, the barn, and even down the road. We had taught Wolfie to always walk off to the side of the road because of the heavy traffic past our house.

We had a saying at our house: "If it's possible to do, we can teach Wolfie to do it." I think the trick we enjoyed the most was when we would pull a chair from the table and call, "Come, Wolfie, it's time to pray."

He would sit up in front of the chair, cross his paws, and lay them on the chair. Then he would lay his head on his paws and close his eyes.

I can still picture that day when near tragedy struck. Papa had just arrived home, and Keith, Earl, and I were helping him unload the car. Wolfie was walking off one side of the road, almost to the house, still looking for his mother.

Suddenly a car came speeding down the road. The young man driving swerved the car off the side of the road, ran over Wolfie, pulled the car back onto the road, and continued to drive toward the little village of Croton, three miles east of our house.

We were sure Wolfie was dead. With anger and tears, Keith, Earl, and I rushed to where he lay, bloody and whimpering. By some miracle, he was still alive.

Papa thought he was dead also, so he jumped into the car and followed the young man who had deliberately run over Wolfie. He caught up with him at the sharp curve, just before you needed to slow down and cross the old bridge before going up the hill and down into the village. He saw the young man pull the car into the churchyard and go inside the church, where a funeral was in progress.

Papa just turned around and drove home. He told us, "The young man must have lost someone very dear to him to cause him to take his pain out on an innocent dog."

My brothers and I were angry. Even though Mama and Papa had taught us that revenge belongs to God, it was still hard for us to just let it go as Papa had done and be thankful that Wolfie was still alive.

A little later, Papa checked Wolfie again and shook his head. "I don't think he can make it," he said. "I'm sorry, kids, but I think it's cruel to let him lie here and suffer. We need to . . ."

Earl and I both knew that if anyone could change Papa's mind, it would be Keith. He had a special way with Papa, and the rest of us children often called him Papa's Little Angel. So when Keith jumped up and placed himself between Wolfie and Papa, we just stood back.

"No, Papa, no!" he pleaded. "I won't let you! He deserves a chance. Mama already has the bleeding stopped. Please, Papa!"

Papa looked at Mama, and she nodded her head. It was settled. Wolfie would have a chance to fight for his life.

And fight he did. Soon he was up walking again. None of his bones had been broken, and the raw wounds were healing, but Mama was unable to save his left eye.

A short time after Wolfie had recovered from his injury and losing his left eye, he was called upon to walk that same road he had walked before while desperately searching for his mother. But this time he was searching for a little lost boy.

My oldest sister, Eleanor, lived with her family just about a mile west of our house on the same road. Her children had been playing outside when suddenly they realized Frankie was missing. He was probably only three or four years old. They searched the house, the barn, and even next door where the uncle lived. Where could he be?

Then one of the older children said, "Maybe he went to visit Grandma and Grandpa." They hurried to our house. "Did Frankie come here?" they asked.

"No," Papa answered, "but maybe we better check along the road. With this traffic you can't tell. I'll take Wolfie with me and check along one side of the road, and you kids take the other side." I had never seen Papa so worried.

We all walked to Eleanor's house. Thankfully, we found no little Frankie on the side of the road. But where was he? It was time to call the police for help. Then his mother decided to try one last hope. "Honk the car horn," she said.

Then from way out in a field of tall grass came a tired little boy rubbing his eyes.

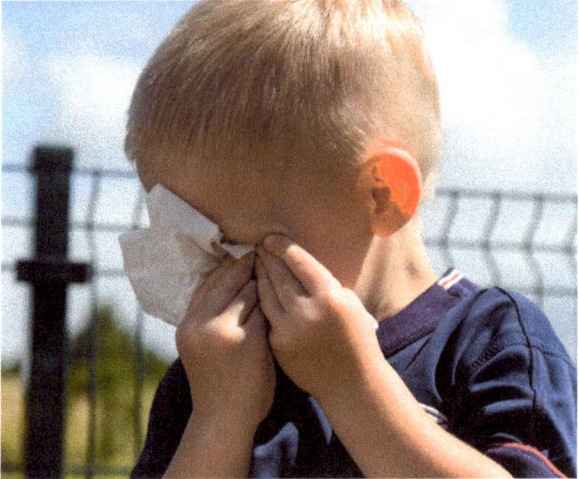

"I tried to catch that chicken," he said, "but she kept running away from me. I got so tired I had to lie down. You honked. Where are we going?"

Frankie got a lot of hugs and kisses that day, but none as sloppy as the kisses he got from Wolfie.

Wolfie and I spent hours together roaming the woods and following the Muskegon River that flowed past our property. We always had to be home in time for him to bring the goats back to the barn. If I tarried too long, he would leave me to bring the goats to the barn for Keith to milk and then come back and walk me home.

When Papa sold all the livestock and then the farm, I hated it. I was in the middle of my junior year at Newaygo High, and I didn't want to move. I loved that old river and the island where the morel mushrooms and the wild leeks grew. I knew that Big Rapids was a much larger school than I was used to, and the thought of all those new classmates terrified me.

Papa did make things a little easier for me. He arranged for me to stay with one of my married sisters until I finished my junior year at Newaygo.

When school was over that year, I rejoined my family at the new farm near Big Rapids. It too had lots of woods, but no river—just some creeks and three little ponds back in the woods. This new farm also came with four or five head of cattle. This was just what Wolfie needed. He had graduated from herding goats to herding cows. He was happy again.

Wolfie and I renewed our friendship and explored this new place together. All 160 acres. As we sat above the three ponds and watched the deer come down to drink, I could feel Wolfie's body quiver as he sat next to me. He really wanted to chase those deer, but he obeyed and stayed beside me. He didn't even bark.

One day I was up in the hayloft, where I often went to be alone and read from Mama's big book of old poems. I heard a noise and turned around. There was Wolfie.

"How did you get up here?" I said out loud. At first I thought Keith or Earl was

playing a trick on me, but they had gone with Papa. Could it be that Wolfie wanted to be near me so much that he had taught himself to climb? Not likely. So I carried him down the ladder and climbed back up myself. He came right up behind me. Later I learned it was Earl who had taught him to climb the ladder.

One day Keith and Earl came home from the woods with a baby squirrel. He had lost his mother. We all took turns feeding him with a doll bottle, and soon he was part of our family. True to his species, he took to hoarding food for a later time in any drawer he could find open. He loved Wolfie and seemed to enjoy riding around on his head and back.

Wolfie was not too happy with this turn of events, but he did allow it. Probably more to please us than himself. But most squirrels need a mother to teach them what foods to eat to supply everything their body needs. It was a sad day, but in the end, Keith and Earl put him in a box and found him a permanent resting place.

Soon afterward, Papa came home with two big puppies a friend had given him—and I do mean big. They were redbone coonhounds. Papa gave Rock to Keith and Zip to Earl. OK, I thought, *now they have their own dogs, so Wolfie is all mine!*

These new dogs grew and grew, and their mouths grew too. You could hear them a mile away. One day Papa and the boys took Rock and Zip to a friend's house to show them off. Sadly, Rock got into some kind of poison and died, but Zip was OK and soon became a part of our family too. Well, almost.

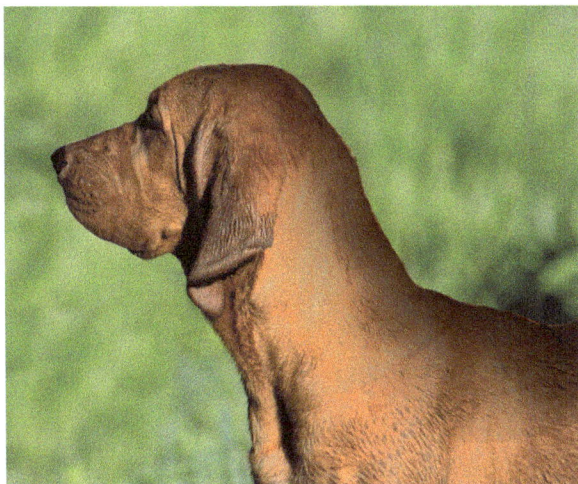

I was so involved with Wolfie at that time that I didn't have room in my heart for another dog. Zip would go with us on our walks through the woods, but Wolfie would never allow him to walk ahead of us or beside me. I knew it wasn't fair, but I allowed Wolfie to get away with it. Even when Zip was twice the size of Wolfie, he never fought back. Wolfie had trained him to obey just as his mother had trained him.

As time passed, Wolfie became even more possessive of me. One evening some friends of our family came to visit, and one of them sat on the sofa next to me. Instantly Wolfie jumped up between us and growled at the young man. The young man didn't think it was funny, but Papa did. Papa thought it was so funny that quite often he would sit beside me and act like he was going to touch me just to see Wolfie jump between us and growl at him. Then Papa would laugh and pat Wolfie on the head. "Good boy, Wolfie, good boy," he would say.

I graduated that June, and just when life seemed so beautiful, tragedy struck again. Our cows ate some frozen plants that caused them to bloat up and gasp for air. Papa was gone, and my older brother Gorden and I didn't know what to do. We had no phone, and our house was the last place on the road. We were a half-mile from the nearest neighbor, and he wasn't home! So we tried different remedies that we had heard about. We must have made those cows run two miles around the barnyard hoping to get rid of the bloat. We did manage to save two of them, but we lost the rest.

When Papa came home and learned what had happened, he blamed himself for not being there. He sold the remaining cows, and we never owned another one. But now we had another problem. Wolfie went looking for the cows the way he had gone looking for his mother back at Newaygo. Finally, he gave up his urge to herd—or so we thought.

One day our nearest neighbor came to our house and told Papa our dog had been killing his sheep. Not Zip, but the smaller one. We knew Wolfie would never, ever harm any of those sheep, especially the little lambs. The neighbor explained that Wolfie had been bringing his sheep from the pasture to his barn almost every night. He admitted he hadn't actually seen him kill any of them, and we couldn't find any wool in his teeth, but we did promise to tie him up until we could teach him to stay home.

We thought we had done that. Wolfie had always been an obedient dog, but the urge to herd must have been just too strong to resist. Late one afternoon, he came home and crawled under the back steps, where the boys had made him a snug house filled with straw. He had been beaten so badly that he died.

When Mama told me what had happened to Wolfie, I was so upset and angry I had to get away. I headed for the woods, but not before I heard Mama say, "Audrey, remember revenge belongs to God." Mama and I were so close to each other that often we knew what the other was thinking before we spoke. Right then she knew my heart and my thoughts better than I did.

Just before dark, I found myself sitting on the hillside beside our property line fence, where Wolfie and I had often sat watching our neighbor's flock of sheep down in the valley below. This was where Wolfie had found sheep to replace the cows. I blamed myself for taking him there. If only I had gone north instead of south. If only I could get even.

The war that was raging in my heart went back and fourth. "Revenge belongs to God." I knew that. But what about Wolfie? He hadn't done anything wrong. I had almost always listened to Mama, and I knew she was right, but what about our neighbor? Was he going to get away with what he had done?

It never entered my mind that he might not be guilty. It had to be him. There was no one else around. But he was such a good neighbor, and my two brothers and I had often warmed ourselves by his fire while waiting for the school bus when it was snowing and blowing outside. I wanted to go to his house and scream at him, but I didn't dare. Suddenly, I was afraid of him.

As I sat there, I felt a cold, wet nose pushing under my arm and pressing against my body, just as Wolfie had always done. It was Zip. He had followed me. "Oh, Zip," I moaned. "You miss him too, don't you?"

As Zip pushed closer, I buried my head against him, and the anger turned to tears. The Holy Spirit, the voice of my mother, and this dog that I had shut out were now helping me to win victory over the demons tearing at my heart.

I never saw or talked to our neighbor again. Papa sold the farm, and we moved a few miles south to a new place. In my heart I knew I had to forgive that man, even if he was guilty—and I did. I even came to the point where I could feel sorry for him. If he really was guilty, he must have had his own demons to contend with.

I must admit, though, that I felt great satisfaction when Papa told me Wolfie had been exonerated. In talking with one of our other neighbors, Papa had found out that our neighbor had caught his own big dog killing his sheep!

That was a great day for me, but I can't help thinking that it will be an even greater day when God Himself will be exonerated, and all, even Satan and his angels, will bow and confess that God is just (Isaiah 45).

We invite you to view the complete
selection of titles we publish at:

www.TEACHServices.com

Scan with your mobile
device to go directly
to our website.

Please write or email us your praises, reactions, or
thoughts about this or any other book we publish at:

TEACH Services, Inc.
PUBLISHING
www.TEACHServices.com ● (800) 367-1844

P.O. Box 954
Ringgold, GA 30736

info@TEACHServices.com

TEACH Services, Inc., titles may be purchased in bulk for
educational, business, fund-raising, or sales promotional use.
For information, please e-mail:

BulkSales@TEACHServices.com

Finally, if you are interested in seeing
your own book in print, please contact us at

publishing@TEACHServices.com

We would be happy to review your manuscript for free.